Thoughts of a Warrior

Volume 1

Beneath the Tracksuit

Robert Gillett

I dedicate this book to
every single person who Is
struggling, fighting, living, surviving
any debilitating lifelong disability.

You are not alone!

Having a disability
may make you feel weak,
However,
It takes a strong person to live with a disability.

First I want to thank you for purchasing my book.
Living the life I live and being able to release a book that I have written myself is an achievement I would have never dreamt possible.

I am not a doctor and I'm not going to tell you what medication you need to be on or what special diet you should eat. I am not here to tell you how to live your life. I'm certainly not Doctor Sningulflerp with a miracle herbal cure.

I am just me, these are my thoughts and this is my life.

The poems and stories I have written in this book all come from my own opinions, my personal struggle, my own experiences from living a life with Depression, Anxiety and Multiple Sclerosis.

Intro

I am Robbie, 33 years old. I am a father, a husband, a brother, a son and a MS Warrior. I am the mind behind Beneath the Tracksuit.

Beneath the Tracksuit is the name for my poetry page, my label or stage name, Whatever you want to call it. I write honest, relatable poetry all about life living with Multiple Sclerosis and living with an invisible illness.

I started writlng poetry after a bad bout of depression. It definitely changed my life, you could even say it saved my life. I battle depression all the time, Different severities of depression at different times, it's always there I'm always fighting, I suppose the fight never stops.

I'm sure MS (Multiple Sclerosis) and depression are best friends.

During this one particular bout I was advised by my Doctor to take antidepressants and go and see a counsellor. Antidepressants I had been on before I had no problem with that. Counselling was good for me, someone I could just rant to and they tried to help with the mess that was inside my head. It can be quite a mess up there.

My counsellor suggested I write a thought diary.

"Why not" was my answer.

I struggled with it. Writing a diary then reading it is so depressing. It wasn't helping. Ok, ok, if you're depressed you probably shouldn't read your daily thought diary which is sad and depressing but I was depressed. Nothing was helping. I was on a roller coaster of self sabotage, constantly beating myself up, telling myself how much of a let down I was, telling myself I was useless. I was literally tearing myself apart from the inside.

A thought diary to write down my daily thoughts was supposed to be a release. The problem with my thought diary is that I didn't give it context.

Mon: I'm sad
Tues: I'm depressed
Wed: I'm stupid
Thur: I'm a let down
Fri: I'm annoyed, sad, angry.

You get the picture.

So what if I put my own spin on it, give it some context, some meaning. What's annoying me? Why am I sad? Why am I depressed?

Make it rhyme, like a rap? Jelly Roll does it. He's an American country rap artist. I found his music in my darkest hour. I found him so Inspirational! So if he can turn his pain into awesome, why can't I? Lots of people do it, singers, song writers, artists, painters, poets, spoken word artists, the list goes on.

So why can't I?

Well I can't paint or draw and you really don't wanna hear me sing. Rapping? Maybe 10 years ago, but poetry is something I can do, so I started.

At first it was embarrassing, seriously. What 30 year old sits down and writes his thoughts and emotions into poetry? That was my head space for a while but I still felt the need to do it.

So I'd write daily, like a thought diary but I'd make verses, make poems, read it over and over but I wasn't taking negativity from what I was reading. I was taking positivity from my sad, broken words. I had made something good, something I could treasure. It was helping, like my little fix I needed to get me through something, instead of running for drink, drugs, fast irresponsible living which I went to many times over the years. I had spent much of my life living with depression and MS only made this worse, but now I've something that actually helps. I'm not hurting myself or anyone around me. I'm just recording my life, my feelings, in a positive way, with so much pain.

Sharing it?

No No No No No!

That was my answer when my Mrs suggested it. These are my personal feelings, emotions, my life. Would you share your thought diary? Not many people would. After a while suggesting it could help other people understand, it could raise awareness for MS and depression, it could help other sufferers, it could let them know they are not alone….

I agreed.

Nervous but I agreed.

Now, a year since I started sharing, my poems are read worldwide. I've had hundreds of people thanking me for sharing. It is definitely worth it.

I didn't write for sharing. These words are my pain, these words are what I write when I am struggling, when I'm suffering, but they relate to countless people. My words are helping others. 18 months ago I was contemplating suicide because I couldn't handle life, I couldn't handle the change I was going through. I couldn't handle the position I found myself in, having to adjust my life to this disability. I've now found myself living in a form of acceptance with MS. So I'll say it again you could say poetry saved my life.

I'm a writer

I'm a writer, I write for me,
I write to express my pain.

Life gets to me, my illness does too,
So putting pen to paper,
Really helps explain.

I write when I can't find the words,
I write to feel safe.

Putting words together, for me,
In my own little space.

I write when I'm happy,
I write more when I'm broken.

Here I find the words,
The words that need to be spoken.

When I write, I become someone new,
I become free.
I take the pain from my life,
Turn it into something of beauty.

I see words,
I see my future brighter,
I found myself at peace,
The day I became a writer.

Being Diagnosed

In March 2015 I was diagnosed with Multiple Sclerosis. It seemed like it took forever. In March 2014 I started the road to getting my diagnosis. One day I froze at work, completely stuck, I was leant over on top of a wooden unit. I couldn't move, shout or talk. I was absolutely terrified! Between 10 to 15 minutes I was just stuck there. After I managed to get my feeling back I got straight on to the doctors who thought I'd had a stroke.

Then began all these other strange symptoms. my left hand started to curl shut, it was doing it on and off for a few days, it was awful. I'd try to hold it open then it would curl back shut. Weird!

I would get these headaches, they were so bad and they would come on in an instant, they would cripple me for hours. I was walking with a sway, my balance was becoming really sketchy.

All these strange symptoms were happening but each one was short lived so not many people could actually see it happening at the points it did. The doctors couldn't pinpoint what was wrong with me. All these symptoms were atypical of an MS relapse because the symptoms didn't last long. A MS relapse would normally be a heightening of previous symptoms or brand new ones that last over a period of time, but mine were more intermittent.

It took a year to finally get a diagnosis. It's not an easy illness to diagnose. It takes a lot of time and some patience too.

There was so many tests

Ultrasound (normal)
Blood tests (normal)
Eye tests (normal)
ECG (normal)
Evoked Potential test (normal)
Balance tests (balance was awful)
MRI scans (scars/plaques/lesions in brain)
Lumbar puncture (abnormal oligoclonal band) I'll add mine was slightly painful and very uncomfortable.

With all the results together it added up to Multiple Sclerosis. It took a year but finally I had a diagnosis . I was heartbroken and I was so scared but at least I had an answer.

I have Active Relapsing Remitting Multiple Sclerosis, there is a clinical reason for what's been happening to me.

It's not in my head and I am not crazy.

Definition of Disabled

Definition of disabled
"Of someone having a physical or mental condition that limits their movements, senses or activities"

This is me.
Now I'm a disabled man.
Classed by the Oxford Dictionary,
A dictionary that has no feelings,
No emotions,
It does not know me.
Still it's given me a label,
One written in the book which publishes the language we speak,
We read,
We write.
It has taken away my right,
My right to just be me.
In this #bekind world we live in where we should not have a stigma or be labelled,
The Oxford Dictionary gave me one.

I'm Robbie,
The Definition of Disabled.
2022©

This Time

There was no accident,
Not this time,
Friends and Family say "you're gonna be fine",
How do they know?
They're not me!
Is it in my head or just insanity?

There's no denying it,
Not this time,
Not even the doctors can say it's fine.
I froze,
Dead still,
Couldn't even blink.
Am I dying?
A stroke?
What would you think?

A new day,
More tests,
What time?
Needles and scans,
Fluids from the spine!
I'm nervous,
Im angry,
I'm scared to say the least.
What am I fighting?
What is this beast?

Test after test,
I got my results this time.
The problem is me,
I'm broken,
Stupid brain of mine.
It's scarred,
Signals blocked,
It's Multiple Sclerosis.
What now?
How am I going to fight this?

Don't give up,
I need to be strong this time!
Quitting is not an option,
Not when there is a mountain to climb.
I'm frightened and it breaks me
But MS i can beat,
I am a WARRIOR within that nothing can defeat.

This time 2020 ©

Making sense of it

Being a young man diagnosed with a lifelong disease was hard. I was 26, I had a career in front of me, my future was sort of planned out. I was very athletic, a hands-on father, I had a very manual job. My life was good, I was actually really happy, then it all changed and it was probably the hardest thing I've ever had to deal with. The hardest thing I've ever had to accept. Even now I still struggle with what is going on with me. I'm still adapting to the new me and all these different changes I have to make in my life. I'm having to change things up and adapt to new ways the more this disease progresses.

The unknown is very difficult to comprehend. We all live a life not knowing what tomorrow will bring but since having MS I've found an extended fear of not knowing. I've had days with new symptoms just coming from nowhere, double vision, neuropathic pain, drop foot, all these symptoms just came on so suddenly.

Drop foot. I was walking home late one night after being out for a few beers. As I was walking I started dragging my left foot across the pavement, I knew there was something wrong straight away, my poor limited edition batman trainers were starting to scuff! The longer I was walking the worse it was getting, I ended up taking my left shoe off. That way my right side was higher and I began lifting my left foot from my hip. I was telling myself not to panic but how could I not. I'd lost the sensation in my foot. It was dead weight and now I needed to drag it or walk lopsided. Now I have different tools I use to help me walk properly, a foot splint to hold it in place to stop me dragging it. I have a walking stick to help keep my balance. I got to use these for life now.

It was as random and as quick as that, it never got better.

It never will.

Most MS symptoms can come on as quick as that and that is scary, no matter how you make sense of it. This is why the fear of more is always sitting in the back of my mind. I know I shouldn't think like that but sometimes it's hard not to.

Comprehend

I've got the symptoms,
I'm feeling the pain,
My doctor has the results,
He sits me down to explain,
"You have Multiple Sclerosis"
"Your final scans have confirmed"
Now I've been given this label,
It's not something I've earned.

I get advice and leaflets,
The number for a nurse,
That's just the beginning,
Now I have fight,
Now I have to accept this curse.
How?
Why is this happening?
What am I going to do?
Do I just have to deal with it?
Do I just have to pull through?
Is this something I just have to accept?
Living life with an illness not knowing what to expect.

There's treatment for the illness,
There's tablets for the symptoms,
Tablets for the pain,
But no-one tells you how to accept an illness,
This illness that's destroying your brain.
My friends can't help,
My family don't understand,
There's no answer for this,
My doctor doesn't have a plan.
The illness is progressive,
The journey doesn't have an end.
How am I supposed to accept this?
That's something I can't comprehend....

Comprehend
2021©

No Words

There's no pain in a leaflet,
There's just words,
There's no emotions in a textbook,
Only information,
You don't understand unless you live with it,
M.S,
This aggressive abbreviation.

How much it hurts,
The doctors don't really know,
The pain it is to live with,
The specialists don't understand,
No-one truly knows how to fight this,
I'm not even sure if I can.

An illness with a thousand symptoms,
How it starts?
No-one can explain!
No-one can tell me why this disease is destroying my brain.

Now I'm stuck with this fear,
I don't know what will happen next,
No-one does!
No-one knows how far it will progress.

I might deteriorate slowly,
I could relapse tomorrow,
I try to live for today,
Still scared for the days that follow.

October 2021
No words ©

No-one sees

No one sees the pills,
No one sees the meds,
No one sees how many times a day I need to go to bed.

No one sees me fall,
No one sees me ache,
No one sees my spasms or sees my body shake.

All this is hidden,
It's not something your eyes just see,
There's not many people who can see my disability.

The smile on my face,
Is hiding all my hurt,
It's hiding all the pain,
Still if someone asks,
I just tell them I'm OK.

The electric shocks,
The burning on my skin,
All of the trouble going on deep within.

No-one sees how much I'm really struggling.
Trying to describe it,
Is to difficult to explain,
I find it too hard to understand!
It drives me completely insane....

I know I am not alone,
There are so many people like me,
Living life as normal as we can,
Whilst fighting a hidden disability.

No-one sees
2021©

People

Dealing with illness is one thing, dealing with other people is a completely different problem. People you have known for years, members of the community and family members all now start to look at you differently. Some are very supportive, I can't thank these people enough, somebody that will listen to you, help you on a daily basis, generally just be there for you. If you are in a position similar to mine, these are the people to hold close.

On the flip side to these lovely people there can be a lot of thoughtless, disrespectful, rude people. I have had some mean things said to me, about me, this is hard. It's hard to try and brush this off and move on from it.

"You're a fraud"
"You're just faking it"
"You're just pretending for the money"
"You're just lazy"

Being sick has in no way made me financially better off, I had to give up the dreams of buying a house, running my own business, being able to save money for my children to give them a head start in life. I have no fancy holidays, I don't wear designer clothes. Financially better off? These people have no idea!

Faking it? I miss out on so much, my family does too. We can't do this because dads poorly, we have to leave early because dads poorly. If it doesn't have disabled access or if there's too many stairs we can't go because daddy's poorly. Daddy can't run the sports day race, daddy can't keep up. Why would I fake it?

You also have the people that are uneducated on the matter. This is something I can understand more. I knew absolutely nothing about MS before I was diagnosed. There are of course absolutely lovely people who take the time to ask the right questions and be very supportive. There is a minority of people who can be very judgemental and really be quite offensive in a way that is really uncalled for.

MS, Fibromyalgia, Functional neurological disorder, Depression, Alzheimer's, any illness you can't see can be very difficult to understand. Most of the world is uneducated on this. It's a case of not knowing unless you have had it impact your life or you are being open to finding out about it.

Maybe people need to not be so quick to judge, take a minute to think before speaking out of turn against someone. It can be very demoralising and emotionally painful when you have people look down at you or question whether you are ill or not.

I fight Multiple Sclerosis,

If I didn't tell you,

You would never know!

Oddity

When people look at me,
I wonder what they see,
Is it the rough road man exterior?
Or my broken body beneath?
Do they notice a look on my face?
Can people see the pain in my eyes?
Do they not notice anything?
Is it all just in my mind?

A young man in a Tracksuit,
A walking stick in my hand,
Discomfort running through my body,
My legs are not letting me stand.
Maybe I look like a joke,
Are these people amused?
Is it because my appearance is strange?
Are these onlookers confused?

Why do I think they judge?
Surely it's not all in my head,
Sometimes I hear them talking,
I catch the whispers that they've said.
I don't like the feeling of the stares,
I'm really not an oddity,
I know people might struggle with it,
I just want them to see me as me.

Oddity 2022©

Fraud

I feel I don't fit in society,
Some people call me a fraud,
They see a smile on my face,
Then "I'm not sick anymore".

I can't help it,
I'm under the covers one day,
Smiling the next,
It doesn't mean I'm faking it,
It means I'm trying my best!

I'm ill on different levels,
Different days,
But I'm always ill,
Just in different ways.
Different pains,
Different aches,
Whatever ability MS chooses to take.

It's hard for me,
I don't know how I'm going to feel today,
Tomorrow,
The day after that,
Multiple Sclerosis is too unpredictable,
For some that makes me a fraud,
But for me,
This is a fact.

Fraud Nov 2021 ©

Man in the Mirror

I wake up in the morning,
Get dressed,
Look in the mirror and I'm shocked at what I see,
Who is this man staring back at me?
The man in the mirror doesn't look like he's in a fight.
I'm confused,
Somethings not right,
He is happy and smiling,
I don't feel that way.
I'm an ill man,
I'm an ill man everyday.
The man in the mirror doesn't look like he's struggling,
He looks well,
He isn't feeling my pain.
I need to check back over and over again.
My image really does contradict the way that I feel.
Surely the man looking back at me,
He can not be real.
When others see me do they see this man in the
mirror?
Is this the image they perceive?
No wonder they don't see my illness,
When I find it hard to believe.

Man in the mirror 2021©

Beneath The Tracksuit

People judge and people stare,
They don't know my situation,
Most people don't seem to care,
They would have filthy looks on their faces,
They look and they say,
"Why is this lad parking in a disabled bay?"
A young man,
A tracksuit,
A cap on my head,
Should I look different?
Should I look older instead?

I'm achy,
I'm broken,
My walking is short,
Disability shouldn't have a stigma,
That's what we have been taught.

I have a stick,
A scooter,
Use a wheelchair,
I have tablets and treatment,
My illness is there,
My pain and my problems are all out of sight,
You can't see them so question you might.

Invisible illnesses are here,
They are real,
For myself and many others we keep them concealed,
I'm young,
I have a disability,
I know it's hard to compute,
But you don't know the struggle
Beneath The Tracksuit.

Beneath the Tracksuit 2021©

I'm Sorry

Why am I always sorry,
Most of the time I feel I do nothing wrong,
Then why do I apologise?
Maybe it is me all along.

I'm sorry to my wife and my kids,
when I need to go to bed,
My head is killing me and my legs feel like they are lead.

I'm really sorry at my appointments
because I'm always running late,
It took me ages to get ready and my head gets in a
state.

I'm sorry I zoned out when people are in deep
conversation.
They need to repeat what they were saying,
My attention runs off,
It's a game my head likes playing.

I'm sorry to the man in the shop because my martkart is
in the way,
This thing is just huge,
I struggle to walk but this makes it easier to move.

When someone has asked me to do something,
I'm always sorry I forgot,
I can't explain why I do this,
But I do this alot.

I'm sorry when I fall,
Sorry when I trip,
I'm sorry when I lose my keys and put the cups in the fridge.

I'm sorry for a lot and sometimes I feel bad,
But most of these problems,
They're caused by the illness I have.

I'm sorry 2022©

Poorly Man

When I was young,
My eyes just learnt to see,
I would notice everything,
I'd notice so easily,
My Mum would say "Its rude to stare"
"He's just a poorly man in his wheelchair".

As I got older,
The questions began to grow,
When i see the poorly man,
I just wanted to know,
How come people get like that?
Why is he so sick?
What happened to him?
How come he uses that stick?
Parents say "you're too young to understand"
I was sad,
I felt bad for that poorly man.

Now I'm an adult,
I see the poorly man across the street,
He's struggling,
He's tired,
He's trying to stay on his feet,
I look at him,
He looks back,
I quickly look away,
Hoping he didn't see me because I wouldn't know what
to say.

Grandparents are normally the nicest,
They are usually quite sincere,
They feel bad for the poorly man,
They will make their feelings clear.

One day it hit me,
It really made me think,
How much life can quickly change,
It only takes a blink,
The children watch my scooter,
Some people see me struggling to walk,
Others stare and quickly look away,
I guess they don't want to talk,
This lady came and spoke to me,
She was older than my mum,
"It's a shame what's happened to you"
"You really are too young"

It took a bit of time,
But now I finally understand,
The reason they all look at me,
I've become that poorly man.....

Poorly Man
September 2021 ©

Thank you

Most people try to be nice,
Some try to tell me what to do.
I should have a different answer,
But I find myself saying thank you.

"You don't look sick"
"You look good"

Thank you!

"You're going to be ok"

I just say thank you.

A quick answer,
Sometimes it's easier that way,
Sometimes I haven't got the energy for what I really
need to say.
I may look good but I feel like death,
I don't look sick but I feel I'm dying,
If I was going to be ok,
Then why am I always crying?

"Have you tried a smoothie?"
"Have you tried watching what you eat?"
"I know how you feel"
"Try taking some time off you feet"

If I thought a smoothie would fix it,
Don't you think I'd drink it?
I'm grateful for your advice,
but it really won't be useful.
You DON'T know how I feel,
This has never happened to you.

I try hard to get better,
I couldn't possibly do any more.
This illness is lifelong,
I can only dream of a cure.
I love how people are optimistic,
I'm grateful that people care,
It's hard for them to understand,
Because this illness
We do not share.

Thank you. 2021 ©

Am I Invisible?

When did I become invisible?
I have a hidden illness but I didn't disappear.
People used to stop and talk to me,
But now they pass me by.
WHY?
It's not like they can't see me,
I stand about 5 ft 6,
In my scooter I'm 3 ft 4,
Did I turn invisible or don't people wanna talk to me anymore?

Are they embarrassed by me?
Do they not know what to say?
I'm still me,
I just live my life a different way.
People show who they truly are when your life gets hard,
Even friends and family stop asking how you are.

Are they fed up hearing the answers?
Have they just heard it all before?
People behave like I'm not here anymore!

I can't get my head around it,
I didn't change,
My personality is still weird,
Honest,
Loving,
It's always been the same.

My abilities may differ,
My needs become additional,
You can't see my illness,
But it didn't make ME invisible.

Am I Invisible ©
Jan 2022

Real

If you can't see it,
Does it mean it's not real?
Look at time,
Oxygen,
Internet,
All real
We know they are real.

Anxiety,
Depression,
Autism,
All real.
Cannot see them but all real.

MS,
FND,
Fibromyalgia,
Cannot see them,
It doesn't mean they're not real.

Invisible illnesses are real,
There's too many to name.
There are millions of people fighting daily,
Living a life of pain.
Being invisible doesn't mean it's not there.
Fact is,
Invisible illnesses are everywhere.

Real. May 2021©

My illness will not stop me from being me!

Negative or judgemental people will not stop me from being me!

The horrendous journey I have been forced to walk on will not stop me from being me!

Fighting the beast

Fighting. Most days I feel that's all I do, I write a lot about fighting. Many people with illnesses describe life being a fight. It's a fight to get out of bed, it's a fight to get dressed, it's a fight with your mental health. It can feel like you're always fighting. Nobody can see the fight, you can't see what goes on inside anybody's head, so why would someone see what goes on in yours? Most people can only see what you show them. No-one is ever really going to see the fight and if they did see you fighting they would never properly understand. I could explain but trying to describe it is too difficult.

I don't know how I'm ever going to feel, physically or mentally, so I fight to keep the negative out of my life. I fight these depressing, anxious thoughts daily. This is probably my biggest fight. That fact my legs might give way in a minute or I might be too tired to carry on my day only feeds the depression.

Fighting the physical side of MS, I suppose with any illness, is hard, mentally exhausting and frightening. I feel myself getting weaker. I struggle to carry my children, play fighting is a non starter. Carrying the shopping became difficult. As a man watching his wife do all the shopping, carrying, lifting, it's heartbreaking, a little demoralising. She's an absolute gem but having to accept that your wife has now taken over your duties and all you can do is pretty much watch, it's difficult.

The symptoms go on forever, well that's what it feels like. From your head to your toes nothing is out of the question because MS affects the brain. In Multiple Sclerosis, Sclerosis means scars in Latin. It literally means multiple scars. They are all in your brain and your central nervous system so it can affect any part of you. Some of the symptoms seem a little far fetched but they are all real.

MS varies from person to person. It's the same as the way the symptoms affect us and how we see and feel them. Here are some of mine:

Dropped foot: I touched on this earlier but this is where your foot stops lifting off the ground. Mine is on my left foot, I have different feelings in both my feet now. It's a bit like saying my foot has gone lazy, it doesn't lift up, I drag it around the house. I trip over anything on the ground because it's hard to step over, stairs are a big problem because I'm constantly kicking the top bit. I can still move it but it's really difficult.

Spasms/tremors: These vary. My legs bounce and shake, my arms gitter and probably the most random one my left kneecap sometimes has a mind of its own and randomly shakes left to right like a nerve is trapped but there's not. They can be annoying but after a while you just get used to it.

Clawed hand/Curled hand: this was one of my first symptoms. My left hand just started curling by itself, like it's trying to grab something. I hold it flat on the wall or floor and the moment I take it off it curls back up. It doesn't happen so much anymore but when I'm having a bad day it can happen or when I'm overly hot.

Headaches: Not just your standard headaches though. They come in different parts of the head with different levels of pain from that niggly one that doesn't shift, to a skull crushing one that feels like someone has hit you with a brick.

Trigeminal Neuralgia: This is a pain I get in my face, the best way to describe it is like having a toothache In the face. The pain is just there, it's painful, it's annoying! There is a reason for this but trying to keep up with the science behind all these symptoms is hard and confusing.

Weakness: Like not being able to lift your arms, your legs won't hold your weight. Being so weak you can't get out of bed, not out of laziness, it's because you have no strength to lift your body.

Neuropathic pain: The wind can breeze across my arm but it feels it's being held over a fire. Cold water can burn my skin, I have different patches of skin that have different sensations to heat and cold.

Diplopia, Double vision: If I overheat or push myself too hard my eyes start to play up, they can malfunction. Then I can get the worst double vision and I have to use an eye patch to bring them back to normal. This is because of leftover damage in the brain from a relapse that left me with double vision for 5 weeks.

Forgetfulness: This can be very frustrating. I'll forget anything, everything, I'll walk into a room and forget why I've walked in there. I'll forget where I'm going, where I've been, what I'm doing. It's a little difficult to understand myself and a lot of the time I second guess myself.

Brain fog: This one can be a little bit amusing. Doing things by accident, putting things where they shouldn't be, seriously no matter how many times I do it the kettle doesn't belong in the fridge, the butter doesn't go in the microwave. Forgetting how to do simple things like how to tie your shoelaces, only for a second and then it comes back.

Pain: I get so many aches, so many different pains. I get pains in my bones, pains and aches in my muscles. It always comes on without a cause but it can feel like I've spent 2 hours in the gym or like I've been in a fight. It can stay around for days or be shorter.

Balance: My balance is awful. It has been as long as I can remember but now it really is horrendous. I have to use a walking stick when I'm out and about, walking only short distances. I furniture-walk around my house. If I find myself in an open space the floor really does become a tightrope. Walking unaided has become a bit of a circus act.

Fatigue: This is rough. It puts an end to most of my days, I struggle trying to manage it. Tiredness and fatigue get mixed up a little bit. Being tired doesn't mean you are fatigued. Fatigue is a whole new level of tiredness, not being able to move your arms or your legs because they are beyond tired. Struggling to lift your body weight, put sentences together, to even think properly. This is more like Fatigue, rather than you can't be bothered to get out of bed or you've been up a bit late, that would most likely be tiredness.

Insomnia: Bloody annoying! When you get so tired, sleepy, you know you need rest but you are still tossing and turning in bed till 3 in the morning. You can not sleep at all. You get so tired but when you get into bed your brain ticks open like you've been drinking coffee but the last cup was 12 hours ago. You just can't sleep. I hate this. I get periods for a few weeks where I'm like this but then fades. Occasionally you get that night where it comes from nowhere and you are all till 4 in the morning for no reason, then it completely messes up the routine the next few days.

Some of these symptoms are just weird.

Here's a hard one for me to tell you.

Urinary hesitancy: I struggle to pee. This is mostly at night but it's easier to handle during the day. You get that feeling you are going to pee yourself, I mean you're bursting so you rush to the toilet and dribbles come out.

You squeeze and squeeze and again dribbles come out, try to sit down, stand up, drink more or less, run the tap, nothing, dribbles come out. This keeps me awake most nights. Highly frustrating! I haven't had a decent pee in over a year. I'm currently on the waiting list for self catheterization.

So to put it straight: On a bad day I'm clinically depressed; I'm confused; forgetful; extra tired and I have a headache; face ache; skin pain; double vision; drop foot; appalling balance and I can't bloody pee.

I don't have all of these symptoms all the time but I do have days when they are all present and these days are the worst. Most days I find myself with pain, aches, neuropathic pain and difficult sorts of headaches.

Everyday I have drop foot, crap balance, urinary hesitancy, brain fog and depression. These daily symptoms never leave and there is no medication for them, this is where adaptations and different tools come into play.

My days may vary but I never feel well, just different levels of disabled.

Fighting all of this daily takes its toll on your body and your mind.

Trying to overcome it is a never-ending fight.

There's plenty more symptoms, the possibility is literally endless. Because the symptoms are caused by getting new scars/plaques in the brain and central nervous system, you cannot rule anything out. I think that's why it frightens me so much.

I try everything.
I keep trying
It's the only way.

Keep positive
Exercise
Good diet
Plenty of rest
Whatever medication and advice the doctors prescribe.

I'm always trying new things to help me along the way. It's about trying to find the right thing for you. I haven't found a permanent fix for me yet but I do what I can to give myself the best chance.

I do my best most of the time and I have periods when I feel I'm winning but I will never completely win because this illness is with me for life so the battle will never stop until they find a cure and find a way to repair the scars in my brain. So the fight goes on and the fight will never stop.

I guess this is why they call us MS Warriors.

"Warrior is a noun that refers to a soldier or someone who is involved in a fight. ...
Today, the word warrior is frequently used to describe a person who is very strong and doesn't give up easily"
Macmillan Dictionary.

Describes me perfectly!

The fight will be hard,

But this fight,

I refuse to lose!

Crumble

I always feel myself beginning to crumble,
But as I start to fall apart,
I dig from deep within me,
I need to fight with all my heart.

I feel the symptoms coming,
They are as terrifying as they were before,
As I begin to give in,
I tell myself I can do it once more.

This conversation keeps repeating,
But I tell myself to stay strong.
This disability is hard,
I need to keep pushing myself along.

The illness never leaves,
It's an ongoing daily brawl,
I never give up the fight,
I am a warrior after all

Crumble Feb 2022

Fighting

Can you see it?
No?
I'm fighting.
I'm always fighting.
Fighting an unseen illness,
Fighting my own thoughts,
It's consuming,
It's frightening.

I live like this daily,
No-one can understand,
I don't look like I'm fighting,
I'm just your average man.
I look in the mirror,
That man lies,
I know I'm getting worse,
I can feel it as days go by.

I know I need help,
But I can be too proud,
It makes me feel weak,
Especially saying it out loud.
I know people care,
I know I'm not alone,
It's still hard to ask for help,
When the demons I fight are my own.

When I look happy,
I have a smile on my face,
What you're actually seeing,
Might not always be the case.
I battle a life with depression,
And an illness you can't see,
No-one else can watch this fight,
I keep it all beneath.

Fighting
2021 ©

A Bad Day

For me a bad day with Multiple Sclerosis is never easy.
I have all the dreaded symptoms,
Not one of which you can see.

My skin is sensitive,
It feels like it's burning!

I have this pain in my arm,
It doesn't stop hurting.

Trigeminal neuralgia is aching my face.

My feet can't hold me up,
I'm falling all over the place.

My balance is terrible,
I'm using my stick to walk.

My speech is stuttering,
I'm struggling to talk.

My brain is confused,
I keep forgetting what to do!

I got this double vision,
Everything I see there is now two.

The fatigue is breaking me,
I should still be in bed.

The depression is crippling,
It's messing with my head.

I'm tripping on my drop foot and the pattern on the floor.

To top it all off,
I can't pee anymore.

It doesn't get easier,
This bad day for me.
Fighting this illness
With symptoms you can't see!

A bad day
March 2022

You've got this

You've got this mate,
You're a fighter,
You know it,
You've got this.

Keep positive,
Stay smiling,
Stay strong,
You've got this.

Absorb the pain,
Stand straight,
Chin up,
You've got this.

Another relapse,
New symptoms,
Don't quit now,
You've got this.

Taking a turn,
Emotionally breaking,
Losing my grip,
Have you still got this?

Dying inside,
You're falling away,
Can't take any more,
I don't know if I've got this..........

You've got this
Nov 21 ©

If I was to tell you.

What If I was to tell you at 25 you were going to have a
life full of upset,
Obstacles,
A lot of pain.
There is nothing you do about it.
It's caused by these new scars,
You've got plaques in your brain.

You feel you're falling apart,
Daily.

You now know at this young age you've actually reached
your peak.

You've worked for a life of strength,
But now you wake up every morning weak,
Not a rough day weak,
Not it's been a long week weak.
You can't lift your arms weak,
Your legs don't move weak.
Now you live broken.

Everyday you will have to fight.
Waking up is a fight,
Getting ready is now a fight.
You'll take a stack of pills,
Attach your armour,
Apply your new gadgets.

This is your fight.
An Invisible Illness destroying you from the inside,
Taking pieces of you,
Your mobility,
Your abilities,
Breaking you,
Inside,
Crippling your mind.

It will slowly take away your light.
All you can do is tread on and fight.

If I was to tell you 2021Ⓒ

Why

Why is it so hard?
Why does this illness have to be tough?
The beating never stops,
I'm always feeling rough.

Bad days turn to bad weeks,
I don't stop feeling ill,
The pain is just to much,
I can't stop taking pills.

The meds take off the edge,
But the pains never go away,
I stay in and lay in bed again,
I've wasted another day.

I lose to much time,
MS takes it away from my life,
I'm constantly struggling,
But I refuse to give up the fight.

March 2021©

The Invisible Thief

If someone was to take something without asking,
They would be a Thief!
You would have someone to blame,
You could do something,
This pain would only be brief.

What happens when they're invisible and they take
something out of you?
What would you do then?
What happens when there is nothing you can do?

Something takes your ability to walk,
Takes away your vision,
Steals your clear thinking,
It holds you into submission,
It tries to take away your life but leaves you living,
Slowly takes away your independence,
Taking the freedom you've been given.

I don't know how you're supposed to handle this much
grief,
Only you have the strength to beat this Invisible Thief .

The Invisible Thief 2021©

The beast

I can't see the beast I fight,
I just know that it's there,
It's always with me,
I carry it with me everywhere.
You can't see this horrid beast,
Its not visible to the eye,
This beast lives within me,
In my body and in my mind,
It tries to take parts of me slowly,
I wrestle with it day and night,
It's a unpredictable beast,
It attacks me unknowingly,
It does it whenever it likes.
I will never stop fighting the beast,
I promise I will never give in,
I will fight this beast all the way to the grave,
One day I will die,
Or just maybe,
One day I'll win.

The beast 2022©

My abilities shrink,

This disease progresses,

Multiple Sclerosis,

The power that it possesses,

Damaging my brain,

But it won't take my mind,

It can't take the power to fight,

That I'm still managing to find.

2021 ©

Depression

This is something I really struggle with. It's so hard to overcome the negative thoughts, the feeling of "being a let down". The fear of disease progression. The fight with myself, I become my own worst enemy.

I have days where I lay in bed hating myself for what I have become, I stand in the mirror and have this shame because of my illness. I get awful mood swings, go from happy, to angry, to moody, to upset all in the space of an hour. I break emotionally at the slightest things and I become emotionless in what would be a happy moment.

Suicide has been a thought that has crossed my mind too many times. The thought of that being the only thing that will fix this for me has been a recurrence in my mind over the years. I know people that have killed themselves and plenty of people that have passed away, what that leaves behind is terrible. I wouldn't want to do that to my family. They have been a rock behind me and they support me all the way through it.

Being a father and a partner can cause my family great upset and confusion in times of my depression but they stick with me and help me through.

I refuse to be beaten by it so I try and I keep trying.

I'm always reminding myself that I am worthy, that I have a beautiful family and that I can have a good quality of life. I have to maintain a level of positivity in my life.

I tell myself, if I needed glasses I would wear them, so why is a walking stick any different? If an athlete needs rest they would take it, so should I. If I want to live healthy I should eat that way, regardless of my illness. It's a constant reminder that this is something I need to do to live my best life.

Of course I still get the negativity and I get it a lot, this is where I like to write about it. I put it onto paper, in my phone and it helps me overcome what's going on in my mind. Everything I write or I have previously written all comes from my thoughts, it's my thought diary, my thought process. Like I said before this wasn't for sharing.

When you're having a bad day,

Remember,

It is okay,

To not be okay!

One day at a time

One day at a time,
I find myself living one day at a time.
I live such an unpredictable life.
With unpredictable symptoms,
Unpredictable emotions,
I never feel stable,
I do whatever I can,
Whenever I'm able.
I never plan too far ahead,
It doesn't sit right in my mind,
I live my life by only taking one day at a time.

Everyday,
Different struggle,
Different daily pain,
Its hard with this illness,
There are no two days that are the same.
I begin my day with apprehension,
Still I start each one as a fresh,
I prepare for the worst,
Can only hope for the best.
What else can you do?
Living with an illness like mine,
Everyday is unpredictable,
So I take it one day at a time.

One day at a time. Jan 2022©

Why Me?

How come I have MS?
What did I do?
Am I just unfortunate?
Is it something else?
Did I do something to bring this on myself?

Why me?
I ask myself this question a lot,
What did I do?
Something I ate as a child?
A substance I misused as a teen?
Sniffed too much glue?
Smoked too much pot?
Probably not.

Why me?
Was I bad in my previous life?
Do I live this hell to pay for it?
Punishment for sins I've committed?
Intervention from a higher power?
Is this why I struggle?
Every day?
Every hour?

Why me?
To test my strengths?
To prove myself as a fighter?
So I appreciate the life I've been taking for granted?
Was this disease given to me because I'm supposed to be strong?
That last question,
Couldn't be more wrong.

I can question why me,
I could find something to blame,
It doesn't do me any good,
It's not like anything will change......

Why me? © Nov 21

How to fix a broken man

How to fix a broken man?
Talk?
Speak out?
That doesn't work.
Kill your self?
Run away?
These won't help,
Get Peace n quiet?
Well done!
Now you're stuck with your thoughts.

How do you fix yourself?
Think of your kids?
Think of your wife?
Think for yourself?
I can't do this.
I'm broken.
Thinking don't help!

Call the helpline!
It's engaged?
Now what?
Listen to music?
Just makes you worse.
Think of past times?
That's what got you here in the first place!

Now what?
Pull your socks up?
Get over it?
Bottle it up?
Have a drink?
Take some drugs?
Crack a joke?
Bury it so deep no one can find it.

Why are you broken?
You have it all?
Great kids,
Wonderful wife,
How can I be broken
I have an amazing life.

How to fix a broken man
February 7th 2021 ©

I wrote this poem in my car, I was in absolute pieces. I had tried to call a suicide helpline and it was engaged. I couldn't believe it. I needed help. No one was there. I was angry, depressed, just so sad. Ending my life was a thought I really had to fight against. I was just broken and I couldn't figure out why. I didn't want to talk to my family because I felt pathetic. I had nowhere to go to talk, so I sat in tears and wrote this.

Within

I'm always trying my best
Happy one day,
The rest?
I'm sick,
I'm depressed.

Sometimes I'm on top of the world,
I love life,
Feel like I'm flying.
Others I want to hideaway,
Feel like I'm dying.

Living like this is hard,
I hope it will one day be easy,
People give me their kindness,
Hoping it will relieve me,

It works for a moment,
Then I end up back where I started,
Sad,
In pain,
Usually broken hearted!

Even with the support around me,
All their comforting words,
Doctors, my family and friends,
No-one can fix the hurt.

I do what I can to move forward,
Not let this disease win,
Show everyone a smile,
Not the hurt within.

Within. Dec 2021©

Best Friend

You were my Best Friend,
You was always there,
You are the one who I trust,
You are the one that cares.

So why are you attacking me?
You've done this before,
This time it's too bad,
I can't take it anymore!

You're picking at my faults,
You're even calling me names!
I'm done with you,
I'm done with your stupid games.

Why won't you leave?
I just can't get away,
I'm sick of you beating on me,
It's every single day.

I fight you,
But you're stronger,
I hide,
Then you find me,
I'd deceive you,
But you're smarter,
I can't escape you,
I need to be free.

How has it come to this?
You're supposed to be my friend.
How is it that death is the only way this will end?

You want to end it,
But I don't want to die.
All I can do is plead,
I keep asking myself why.

As I see you in the mirror,
I tell you I don't want to play your game!
Why do we keep fighting?
We are both one,
We are both the same.

Best Friend 2021 ©

Tears

When my tears roll down my face I wonder what if they had a voice,
Would they tell me anything?
What would they be able to say?
Would they describe my life and tell the story of my pain?
Explain the agony I live with each and every day?

Would they be quiet and tentative and support me through my depressive state?
Would they give me compassion and help me?
Tell me that this time I am not going to break?

Would they whisper about the fear of the future I struggle to see?
Would they be angry from the neglect from the people I have around me?

Would they be loud and give me encouragement to help me through my daily fight?
Would they be proud and tell me to keep going?
Let me know that what I'm doing is right.

I try to hold them back but sometimes I don't have a choice,
As they trickle down my face,
I wonder,
What if my tears had a voice?
Tears 2022©

Around 1 in 5 people of the general population will suffer from depression at some point in their lives. People who fight life long illnesses have a depression rate considerably higher. The demons we fight we generally fight alone, No-one should suffer alone.

Please speak out.

Don't be your own worst enemy.

Please reach out, Seek help, Don't suffer in silence.

New way of life

Now I have this illness, I have this fight in front of me. I have the people I need to deal with, the daily thoughts and the battles with depression. I need to get used to my new way of life, I need to get used to the adjustments I make and new gadgets I get to use.

Walking stick
Functional Electrical Stimulation (FES)
Foot splint
Arm splint
Eye patch
Muscle wraps
Heat pads
Pill box
Mobility Scooter
Mart Kart
Automatic Car
Disabled Access

The list goes on..........

It takes a significant adjustment in your thinking. My way of life completely changed. I now have to remember these things on a daily basis. I need them all at different times for different things and it gets overwhelming. My whole life became different and it's always changing but I adapt, adjust and carry on.

How Many

How many times has depression got you down?
How many times have you had to fight that frown?
How many times does your mind run astray?
How many times do you fall in a day?
How many times has the air burnt your skin?
How many times has it hurt deep within?
How many times has there been a problem with your sight?
How many times has NOTHING kept you awake at night?
How many times have you struggled to talk?
How many times have you been too tired to walk?
How many times a day do you just forget?
How many times a day do you just get upset?
How many times do you feel you might break?
How many different tablets and medicines do you take?
How many doctors and specialists do you see?
How many times do you wish,
Wish you were free?

These questions are real,
They're painful,
They continue to mount,
I can't even answer them,
Years ago I lost count.

How many
2021©

Mart Kart

We've all seen them,
They're always in the way,
I never would have thought,
That would be me one day.

Embarrassing at first,
Now I must admit,
I think they are AMAZING!
They are a smart bit of kit.

That massive scooter,
The one with the basket sticking out,
If you haven't yet,
Try it,
You'll love it,
No doubt.

All those people,
They cannot help but look,
I think they're jealous,
They have to do their shopping on foot.

Who would have known,
It would be this much fun?
I couldn't think of a better way to get the shopping done.

Get the bread,
The milk,
The pasta and the cheese,
I am so fast in the shop,
You wouldn't believe.

My legs barely work,
It does break my heart,
But I do love shopping,
In the chunky Mart Kart.

Mart cart. 2021©

Knock knock

Knock Knock!

Hi mate it is a little late but I haven't seen you in ages,
Did you pop in for a chat?
Just remind me that you're there?
I'd forgotten about you,
Last time you left me in despair.
Next time mate please not at midnight,
I'm always tired these days,
I don't live the same life.

Knock Knock!

You're back,
You're here again late in the night,
You're keeping me awake!
Why? Why? Why?
It's the middle of the week,
Tomorrow I have things I need to do,
Why are you keeping me up?
What are you trying to do?
My eyes were just closing,
I'd almost nodded off,
4 hours of sleep is really not enough.

Knock Knock!

Seriously!
What now?
You bring me pointless conversations and intrusive
thoughts,
Most of the time it makes no sense,
I don't want it anymore!
It's 2 o'clock in the morning,
I just want to get some sleep,
It's not the time to be thinking about our latest world cup
defeat…

Knock Knock!

That's it,
I've had enough!
Not getting enough rest is really becoming tough,
You're disrupting my nights,
It's ruining my days,
I can't handle this INSOMNIA,
You and your tiring,
Pointless games.

Knock knock. Jan 2021

Why am I so tired?

I'm tired
Tired of pain,
Tired of aching,
Tired of headaches,
Tired of decision making.

I'm too tired to think,
Too tired to talk,
Too tired to move,
Too tired to walk.

It's not an excuse,
I'm just tired.
I can't help,
I'm sorry,
I'm just too tired.
I'm not lazy,
I'm just tired.
You don't need to worry,
I'm just so tired.

I don't understand why,
I'm just always tired.

Why am I so tired 2021©

Make MS My Friend

You came to me,
You came to live in my brain,
Why do we constantly hurt one another?
Don't you ever feel the same?

Why do we have to fight?
What if I was to make you my friend,
What if we just stop?
Try to live peacefully until the end.

Instead of seeing you as the enemy,
I can call you my friend Steven,
I don't upset you,
You leave me alone,
We can both be even.

If I treat you with respect,
I'll rest when you need,
Can we live peacefully together?
Would you do this for me please?

We don't have to be enemies,
You don't need to keep hurting me,
If we work together,
Maybe we can live in peace.

Make MS my friend 2021©

Family

My family is the most important thing to me in the world. We are a normal-ish family, we all have our quirks for sure but I wouldn't change a thing.

This illness would be a whole lot harder if I didn't have them around me. I would have made a lot of different decisions, I would have probably drank a lot and would have been more of a mess through my diagnosis. I wouldn't have taken it the way I did and that's for sure. I might have fallen off the rails rather than have periods of depression and struggles with my mental health.

Multiple Sclerosis takes its toll on me and my life but what about the people me?

I have young children, a son and a daughter, who are both absolutely amazing and deal with my illness in such a grown up way. They are both now classed as young carers. They both hold this title proudly.
I have a wife too and she is the most supportive and understanding person I have ever met. I know I'm very lucky to have them all.

My illness affects me physically but it affects them just as much mentally as it does me. My children are growing up and watching me get weaker as time goes on. They see that daddy misses things and daddy can't do certain things anymore.

But they do see him try!

They don't see him quit!

It is scary for them, they've seen me fall down the stairs, trip over in public, they've seen me cry in pain or cry because I'm sad. They watch me crumble midday and go to bed. They watch me struggle but they watch me fight, and support me every step of the way.

They all pull together if I ever need anything or I need any help with anything. They have such a good understanding of what's going on with me. They have a great understanding of what MS means for our little family. We are all in this together and we work as a team to get through it.

They make me so proud.

I really couldn't do my life without them.

Little Brain.

Please little brain of mine,
Could you just give me a break?
I can deal with all the pain you cause,
But now my heart begins to ache!
You've caused me all this damage,
This I can handle,
This I can pull through,
Now you're hurting my family,
I don't know what I can do!

You hurt me and my body,
In so many different places,
This pain is so much harder,
It's the look on all their faces.
They watch on and they weep,
The more I become broken,
I can see what they are feeling,
Without one word being spoken.

They all make sacrifices,
They stand by my side and they love me,
We fight this as a family,
For that I know I'm lucky.
You're not being fair,
You're hurting the ones I love,
Please little brain of mine,
Haven't you done enough?

Little Brain ©

A letter to my daughter.

To my darling daughter.

I know we are in this modern era, we have social media and mobile phones but I wanted to write you a letter. I want to tell you I am so proud of you and I could not have wished for any better.

You are always there for me, you will always help me. You will generally do as I ask. You will help with the rubbish bins, you help with the dishes. You will help with anything I need really, no matter how trivial the task.

You would try to catch me if I fall. You will try to be quiet when I need rest. You really do make us smile the way you always try your best. It must have been so hard having to become a young carer at twelve and looking after your poorly dad. Thank you so much for all your help and making me smile when I am sad.

One Day you will get older, you will leave home and you will be gone. Of course I'll be sad but I'll be so proud of the woman you will become. The man that you marry will be one lucky Groom.

But for now my darling.

Can you please tidy your room?

Love Dad.

Daddy

Daddy, I love you.
I love you to mate,
Are you ok?
I'm fine daddy,
It's your MS that I hate.

Daddy I'm sad when you're poorly,
Do you think they will find a cure?
The doctors are trying their best so one day they will,
I'm sure.

Does it hurt daddy? You're always in pain.
It does sometimes but the medicine takes some of my
hurt away.

Am I going to catch it daddy?
Because I am your son?
You can't catch it mate,
It's not a disease you can pass on.

I'm scared for you daddy,
I don't want you to die.
It's ok,
I'm not going to die,
It upsets me a lot,
That's why you see me cry.

Daddy, if I ask Santa can he take it away?
I don't want presents for Christmas or my birthday.
I could sell all my toys,
I'll even behave better,
I just want to help you daddy,
I want you to be better.
I want you better so we can race,
I want you better so we can run around and play all day.
We can play football,
We could even wrestle,
I want you like that,
Do you remember being that way?

I'm sorry son,
There's no way to make my MS gone.
Don't worry we can still enjoy ourselves,
Be silly,
We'll make it all fun.
We can have a good life and we'll fight this together.
I know we will daddy,
It doesn't matter you're poorly,
I'll still love you forever.

These are some of the conversations that me and my
son have had over the years. The impact of having an
illness has on our children can be so heartbreaking but
we fight together.

Daddy 2021©

Being Grateful

I am so grateful for the lovely family I have around me and the support they have shown me over the years. I am so grateful for the nurses and doctors we have in our country. The world doesn't have the luxury of a health care system like we do here.

Being ill and having to live with MS has taught a few things about life, what's important and what I should be doing with my life.

I am more thankful for what I have in my life and things I can still do instead of focusing on the bad and the things I can't do anymore.

I am grateful for a lot more in my life, I'm doing my best to not take things for granted.

Gratitude and being thankful has helped me realise along the way just how lucky I am. I am ill and I do live with a degenerative disability but there are millions of people that have life worse than me, have a more severe illness than mine.

I may be ill but it could be worse…

You fought yesterday,

You will fight tomorrow,

You survived last year,

You will survive the next,

Believe in yourself,

You're a warrior,

Live your life to its best.

Grateful

You can't have all the things you want,
The stuff you rush to get,
Those material things,
You're in no real need to collect.
A bigger TV,
A faster car,
These things don't make you better,
Better than you already are!
You have clothes to wear,
You have food to eat,
You have drink you can drink,
You have a bed where you sleep.
You have a house you call home,
You might have a car you drive,
You have the luxury to breath,
You are still alive.
Put aside your need for want,
Ask yourself,
What are you grateful for?

Your legs work,
You can walk,
Your eyes work,
You can see,
Your brain works,
You have the power to be anything you want to be.
Don't get stuck in a world of wanting and greed,
Rushing and worrying for things you don't really need.

Be grateful,
Be grateful for your family,
Your friends,
The life that you live,
The love that you receive,
The love that you can give.
Be grateful for your good times,
The recent and the past,
Be grateful for the gift of the present,
Because the present will not last.

Take a minute,
Ask yourself,
What am I grateful for?

Grateful. April 2021

Advice

Now we are getting to know each other,
Can I please give you some advice?
Please don't judge in life,
Always TRY to be nice.

Walk each day with a smile on your face,
Hold your head high,
Anything can happen,
Don't let life pass you by.

Don't be down by the little things in life,
They don't really matter,
They won't in ten years time.

Chase your dreams,
Go for an adventure,
You can do anything you want,
Do something you want to remember.

Go see the world,
You could jump out of a plane,
Think outside the box,
Do something insane.

You could find someone in need,
Show them some support,
Life is precious,
This is true,
Much more than a thought.

You don't know if your opportunities will ever be
snatched away,
Live life to its fullest,
Make the most of today.

Advice 2021©

Thank you

I want to thank you all for taking the time to read my book and going through this journey with me. I hope you take some encouragement from this, maybe some inspiration.

Living with Multiple Sclerosis has been such a challenge for me, it still is, but living with it doesn't mean I have to stop living.

I've spent the last 8 years adapting, changing and fighting my way through my struggles and it's not over yet. I'll continue writing, working with my illness and doing what's right for me, my body and my mental health. I don't have a choice but I'll remember what is important to me. I'll stick with trying to live for the quality of life and do my best to not be anxious about it.

Accepting the illness is difficult, I suppose I'll never really understand it, but I know I have to live with it.

All I can do is fight and do what's right by me and my family.

I Remember

I remember,
I remember running,
I remember climbing,
I remember believing I was unstoppable,
Unbeatable,
Undefeatable,
I was a champion in my own right.

I was brave,
I was strong,
I would work hard,
Train hard,
Accomplish,
Achieve,
Nothing out of reach,
Nothing out of sight.

I could push forward,
Overcome the little obstacles,
Fight to beat the big ones,
Take the world in the palm of my hand,
And tell myself it's alright.

Multiple Sclerosis didn't stop that,
I got sick,
I became disabled,
But Multiple Sclerosis didn't stop that!

It's proved to me I am unstoppable,
Unbeatable,
Undefeatable.
I'm even more of a champion now than I ever was
before.

I'm braver,
Stronger,
I work harder,
Train harder,
I have bigger accomplishments,
Bigger achievements,
I can reach further than I ever did before.

I only move forward,
I move all the obstacles that stand in my way,
No matter how big,
How small,
I have no choice but to tackle them all,
I look at world in the palm of my hand trying to
understand where on this planet I stand,
Not letting it make a difference that I became a disabled
man.

I can't run anymore,
I don't climb anymore,
Unless im picking myself up from the floor,
Or climbing out of the depressive hole I managed to find
myself in,
Again.

I've adjusted my whole life,
My whole sense of being who I am,
Just so I can,

Just so I can be me.

Multiple Sclerosis flipped my life,
Turned it upside-down,
Inside out,
Multiple Sclerosis pulled me apart.
But that was just the start.

My life started over,
It hit the reset button,
The soft reboot of myself,
Adjusting to a life where I now need help,
I need to be real,
Focused,
Concentrated,
I'm living strong,
I have bravery travelling within me,
Reborn to be mightier,
Multiple Sclerosis made me a fighter.
I let nothing get in my way.

I remember running,
But I didn't like to run anyway.

I remember.
Beneath the Tracksuit 2022 ©.

End Note

At the beginning of the book I said it was embarrassing writing poetry.
"what sort of 30 year old man writes down all his thoughts, feelings and emotions into poetry".

Well, it turns out they do. Hundreds of years ago, In the time of the bravest and strongest warriors, A Skald was a poet who would write epic tales and poetry of battles, war and sex from their experiences of war and life. This was a way to record their times and a way to tell others about the life they have been living.

Egill Skallagrimsson
Skald Warrior Poet
910-990AD

'More may yet be told,
An men silence hold:
Further feats and glory,
Fame hath noised in story.

Warriors' wounds were rife,
Where the chief waged strife;
Shivered swords with stroke
On blue shield-rims broke.

Egills saga V.7

Robert Gillett
Beneath the Tracksuit
2022

Printed in Great Britain
by Amazon

79436923R00058